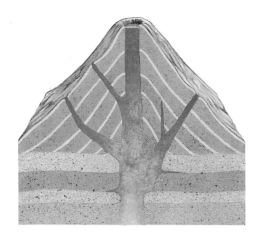
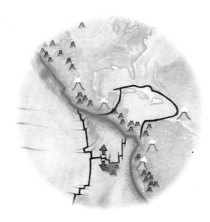

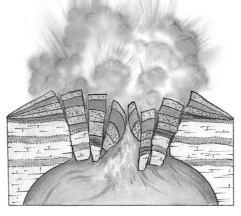

What is a volcano?

A volcano is an opening in the Earth where hot, liquid rock, called magma, bursts out.

When a volcano explodes, it is called an eruption. A volcanic eruption is one of the most powerful events in nature. Hot ash, rocks and gases are thrown high into the air and the sky goes dark. Volcanoes can be many shapes and sizes, and are found all over the world.

A volcanic eruption

When a volcano erupts, lumps of red-hot magma are thrown hundreds of metres into the sky at great speed. Some magma lands more than a kilometre away from the volcano.

Scientist in a protective suit watching a lava flow

Lava flows

When magma reaches the surface it is called lava. Sometimes, lava flows down the outside of the volcano like a river. This river of lava can be hundreds of metres deep. As it cools down, it hardens into rock and stops moving.

My Best Book of

Volcanoes

Simon Adams

Contents

Created for Kingfisher Publications Plc by Picthall & Gunzi Limited

Author: Simon Adams
Consultant: Dr Jon French, University College London
Editor: Karen Dolan
Designer: Dominic Zwemmer
Editorial assistance: Barnaby Harward
Illustrators: Rob Jakeway, Bill Donohoe

KINGFISHER
Kingfisher Publications Plc,
New Penderel House,
283–288 High Holborn,
London WC1V 7HZ
www.kingfisherpub.com

First published in hardback by
Kingfisher Publications Plc 2001
10 9 8 7 6 5 4 3 2 1

1TR/1200/WKT/MAR(MAR)/128KMA

First published in paperback by
Kingfisher Publications Plc 2002
10 9 8 7 6 5 4 3 2 1

1TR/1101/WKT/MAR(MAR)/128KMA

A CIP catalogue record for this book is available from the British Library.

ISBN 0 7534 0550 4 (hardback)
ISBN 0 7534 0633 0 (paperback)

Printed in Hong Kong

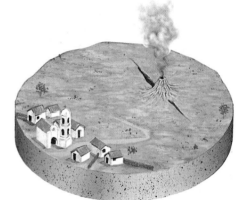

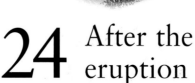

Inside a volcano

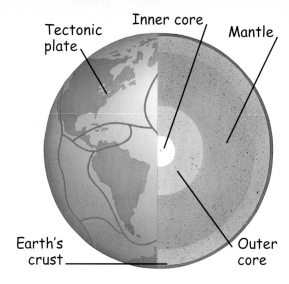

A volcano is made up of long pipes called vents. These vents are connected to a hole deep inside the Earth called a chamber. Inside the chamber there is magma which can be as hot as 1,200°C (water boils at 100°C). The magma rises up through the long vents and comes out on the Earth's surface as lava. There are even volcanic vents under the ocean floor. There, magma comes out of cracks, called fissures, in the ocean crust.

The Earth's layers

At the centre of the Earth is a solid metal core, which is surrounded by an outer core of liquid metal. Around this is a layer of hot rock called the mantle. The surface is broken up into large pieces called tectonic plates.

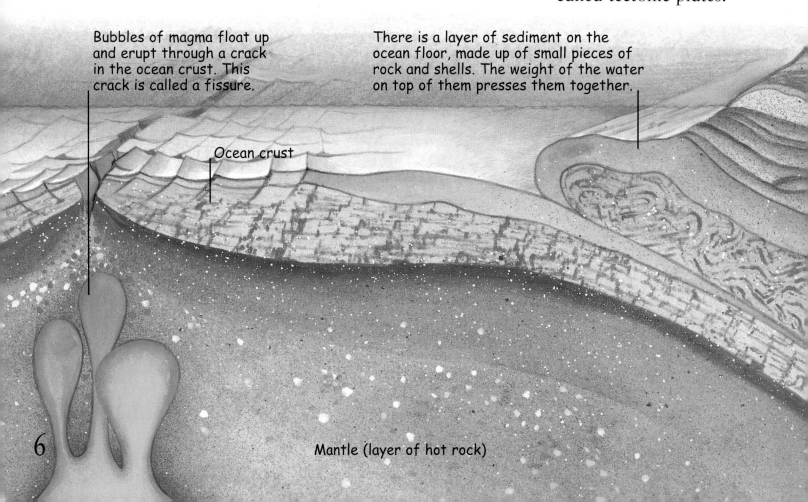

Bubbles of magma float up and erupt through a crack in the ocean crust. This crack is called a fissure.

There is a layer of sediment on the ocean floor, made up of small pieces of rock and shells. The weight of the water on top of them presses them together.

Ocean crust

Mantle (layer of hot rock)

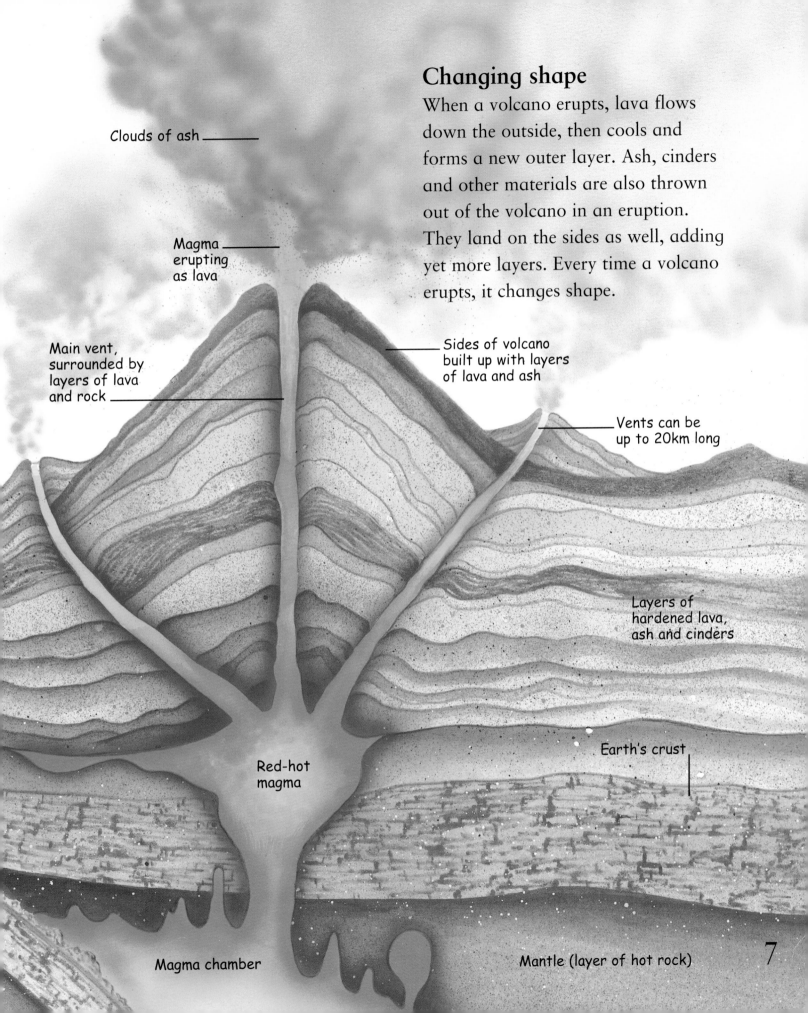

Clouds of ash

Magma erupting as lava

Main vent, surrounded by layers of lava and rock

Changing shape

When a volcano erupts, lava flows down the outside, then cools and forms a new outer layer. Ash, cinders and other materials are also thrown out of the volcano in an eruption. They land on the sides as well, adding yet more layers. Every time a volcano erupts, it changes shape.

Sides of volcano built up with layers of lava and ash

Vents can be up to 20km long

Layers of hardened lava, ash and cinders

Earth's crust

Red-hot magma

Magma chamber

Mantle (layer of hot rock)

Types of volcano

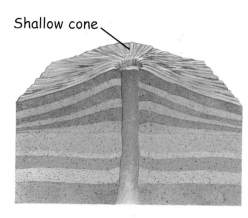

Shallow cone

There are many different types of volcano. A fissure volcano is almost flat, and a composite volcano is tall and steep-sided. The sides of a volcano are usually formed when lava cools into solid rock. But the steep sides of ash-cinder and composite volcanoes are formed when ash and cinders or lava fall outside the volcano, then cool and harden into separate layers.

Shield volcano

Volcanoes in the Hawaiian islands of the Pacific Ocean have runny lava. This lava flows out gently to form a shallow volcanic cone, shaped like a shield.

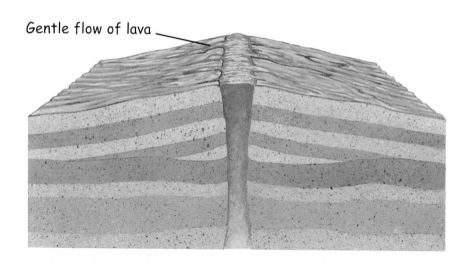

Gentle flow of lava

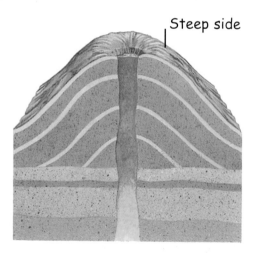

Steep side

Fissure volcano

A fissure is a crack in the Earth's crust. It can measure many kilometres long. Magma erupts through the fissure and flows down the sides of the volcano in little rivers, to form a gentle slope on each side.

Dome volcano

A dome volcano has a single vent, or pipe, from which the magma erupts. Thick, fast-cooling lava flows down the sides of the volcano to form a steep-sided dome.

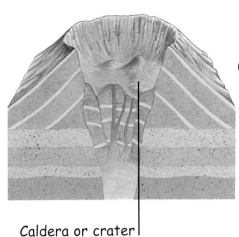

Caldera or crater

Caldera volcano

When the top of a volcano collapses into the magma chamber, it makes a crater, or caldera. Sometimes this fills with water to form a lake.

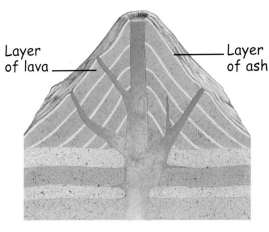

Layer of lava

Layer of ash

Composite volcano

A composite volcano is formed of layers of ash and lava in the same way as an ash-cinder volcano. The sides are steep.

Ash-cinder volcano

When a volcano erupts, the heavy cinders fall on the sides of the volcano first, followed by the lighter ash. After each eruption, layers of cinders and ash build to form a steep-sided cone.

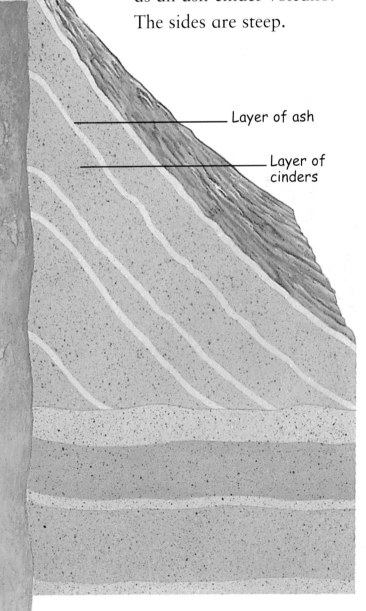

Layer of ash

Layer of cinders

9

Where in the world?

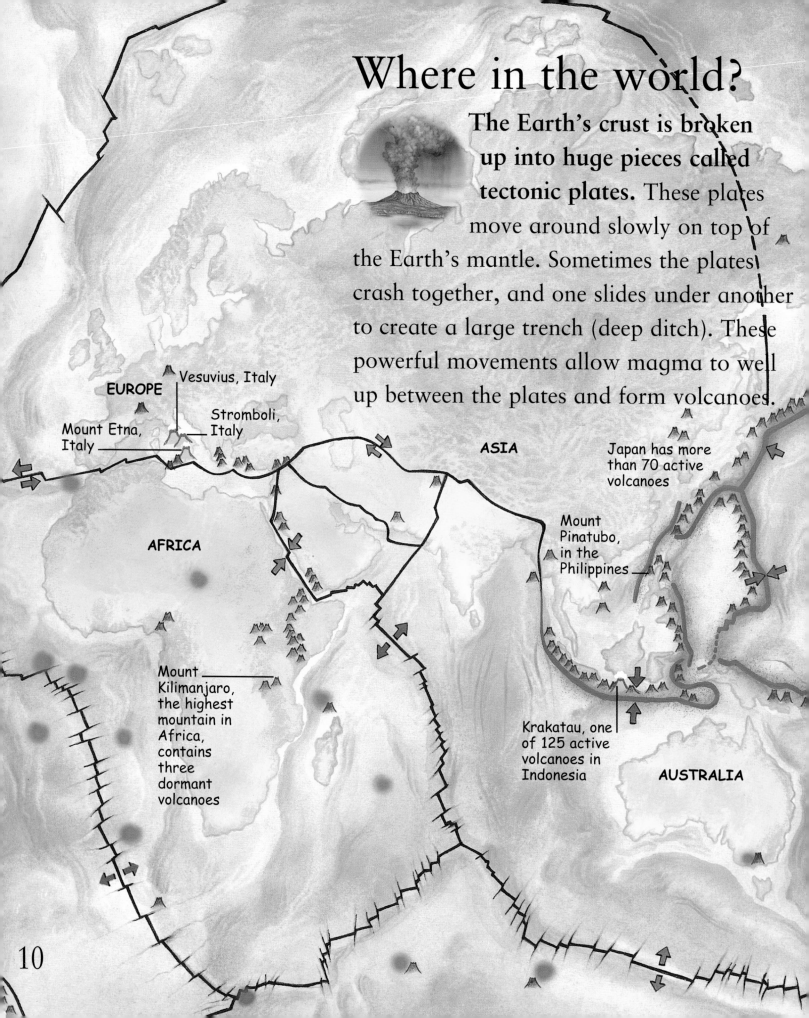

The Earth's crust is broken up into huge pieces called **tectonic plates.** These plates move around slowly on top of the Earth's mantle. Sometimes the plates crash together, and one slides under another to create a large trench (deep ditch). These powerful movements allow magma to well up between the plates and form volcanoes.

EUROPE

Vesuvius, Italy

Mount Etna, Italy

Stromboli, Italy

ASIA

Japan has more than 70 active volcanoes

AFRICA

Mount Pinatubo, in the Philippines

Mount Kilimanjaro, the highest mountain in Africa, contains three dormant volcanoes

Krakatau, one of 125 active volcanoes in Indonesia

AUSTRALIA

10

Ring of Fire

The huge Pacific Plate is moving slowly against the plates next to it. As a result, a chain of volcanoes has formed around its edges. This chain is known as the Ring of Fire. It includes many of the world's most active and powerful volcanoes.

Hot spots

In some places on Earth, the crust is very thin. A hot spot volcano forms when magma pushes through a thin part of the Earth's crust, and erupts onto the surface. Many hot spots are underneath the ocean. Some underwater volcanoes grow to form islands, such as the Hawaiian islands in the Pacific Ocean.

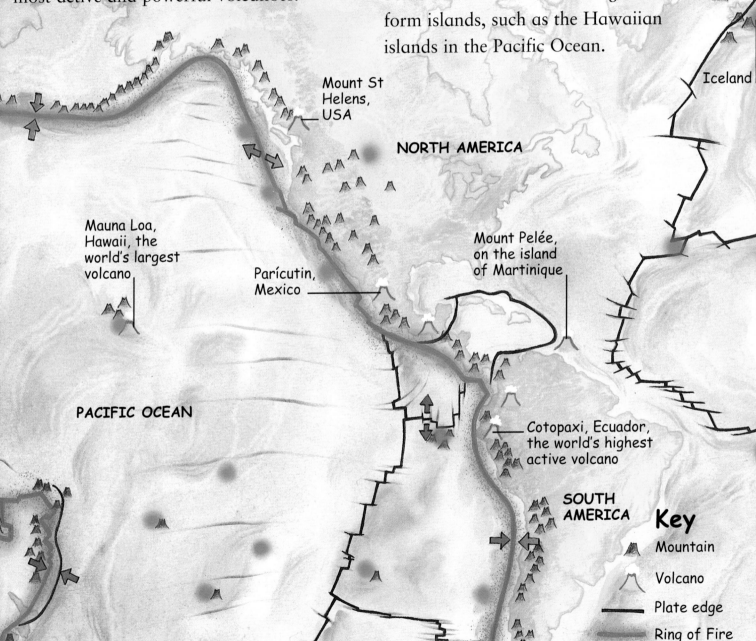

Iceland

Mount St Helens, USA

NORTH AMERICA

Mauna Loa, Hawaii, the world's largest volcano

Parícutin, Mexico

Mount Pelée, on the island of Martinique

PACIFIC OCEAN

Cotopaxi, Ecuador, the world's highest active volcano

SOUTH AMERICA

Key

⛰ Mountain

🌋 Volcano

— Plate edge

— Ring of Fire

⇨⇦ Moving plates

● Hot spot

11

Volcanic eruptions

Volcanoes can be active, dormant or extinct. An active volcano is one that has erupted in the last 10,000 years and will probably erupt again. A dormant (sleeping) volcano might erupt at some time in the future. An extinct (dead) volcano will never erupt again. There are more than 1,500 active volcanoes in the world. Some of these erupt quietly, but others blow their tops in giant explosions, sometimes killing people and destroying whole cities.

Black sky

Mount Pinatubo in the Philippines erupted in June 1991. It threw out huge amounts of ash, dust, lava and dangerous gases that raced down the slopes of the volcano at 100km per hour. Dust and ash turned the sky black and, as they fell to Earth, covered everything with a thick, grey blanket.

Volcanic material

When a volcano erupts, it throws out ash, cinders, and small and large lumps of rock and lava.

Cinders
These are small lumps of rock. Lapilli are smaller stones.

Ash
This is formed of the tiniest pieces of volcanic rock.

Volcanic bombs
These are lumps of lava that form shapes as they cool down.

Pele's hair
These are thin strands of lava, named after Pele, the Hawaiian goddess of volcanoes.

13

Rivers of fire

Some lava is thin and runny and speeds down the sides of the volcano in red-hot rivers. Other lava is thick and sticky, and creeps forwards perhaps a metre or two a day. These slow lava flows are often hundreds of metres thick. They move so slowly that the surface cools and hardens into a thick skin, which breaks up as new lava flows are forced through it.

Mount Etna

Mount Etna, on the island of Sicily in Italy, is one of the highest and most active volcanoes in Europe. Lava often pours down its sides, and ash showers the town of Catania at its base.

Different types of lava

Pahoehoe lava

Pahoehoe (*pa-hoy-hoy*) is a runny lava. As it cools, it forms a wrinkled skin which looks like coils of rope.

Aa lava

Aa (*ah-ah*) is a jagged, crumbly lava formed when molten rock cools down on contact with air.

Pillow lava

When magma wells up under the sea, it cools and forms large bubbles of lava that look like stone pillows.

Crystals and gems

As molten lava cools, the minerals inside it slowly harden into crystals. Some rare and precious crystals, such as diamonds, are cut and polished into gems.

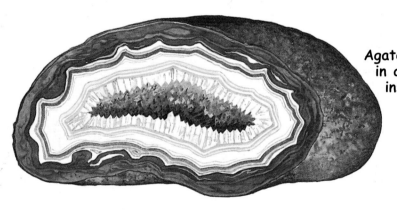

Agate, formed in a bubble inside magma

Zeolite, a glassy crystal of oxygen, silicon and various metals

Olivine, a shiny stone containing iron and magnesium

Cut olivine (peridot)

Uncut diamond in volcanic rock, from the mantle

Cut diamond

15

Volcanic lands

A smoking or erupting volcano shows clearly that magma is rising through the Earth's crust. There are other signs to look out for too. All around, the land bubbles and steams from the heat of the magma. The magma and volcanic rocks heat up underground water, which rises to the surface as geysers, hot springs and mud pots. This heated water mixes with gases to form small vents called fumaroles. Some fumaroles, solfataras, smell like rotten eggs.

Some underground water that is heated by magma escapes in a geyser of hot water and steam. _____

Land of bubbling mud

New Zealand lies on the edge of the Pacific Plate, which is crashing into the Indo-Australian Plate. This means that the island has many active volcanoes, geysers, hot springs, and bubbling mud pots.

Some water heated by magma dissolves the rock, and rises to the surface as a bubbling mud pot full of minerals.

Building a volcano

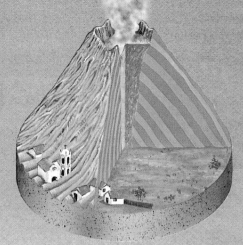

1 The Parícutin volcano first erupted in a field in Mexico in 1943. Within a day it was 10m tall.

2 After a year, many more eruptions had added layers of ash to the cone. It was now 450m tall.

3 By 1952, Parícutin was 528m high and covered in layer upon layer of heavier cinders and lightweight ash.

Some water heated underground by the hot magma rises to the surface in hot springs.

Sulphur fumes from the magma mix with steam from the hot water to form solfataras.

Small vents called fumaroles shoot out hot steam and smelly gas.

Underwater volcanoes

Many volcanoes form thousands of metres under the sea. Sometimes, the seabed slowly opens up as two tectonic plates pull apart, and magma bubbles up through the crack to form a volcano. In other places, the plate is thin and easily broken by columns of hot magma. These are called hot spots. After many years, some of these volcanoes rise above the sea to form islands. Before long, grass and trees grow, and seabirds nest there.

Black sand

Many volcanic islands have black sand beaches. When hot lava hits the cold sea, it shatters into tiny, glassy pieces, containing dark-coloured, or black, minerals.

How a volcanic island is formed

1 A column of rising magma burns its way through a weak spot in the Earth's crust, and erupts on to the sea floor.

2 Over the years, the volcano grows slowly under the sea as more eruptions add layers of lava that make it taller.

3 Finally, the volcano breaks through the surface of the sea, and forms a new island.

Unmanned submarine exploring the ocean depths

Chimneys made of layers of copper, iron, sulphur and zinc

Black smokers

Where gaps form below the seabed, volcanic springs spurt out hot water that is black. This is because it is full of dark-coloured minerals. When this water meets the cold seawater, it hardens and builds up into tall chimneys called smokers.

Giant tube worms feed on bacteria that live inside their bodies

Giant clams can grow up to 30cm long

Volcanic lakes

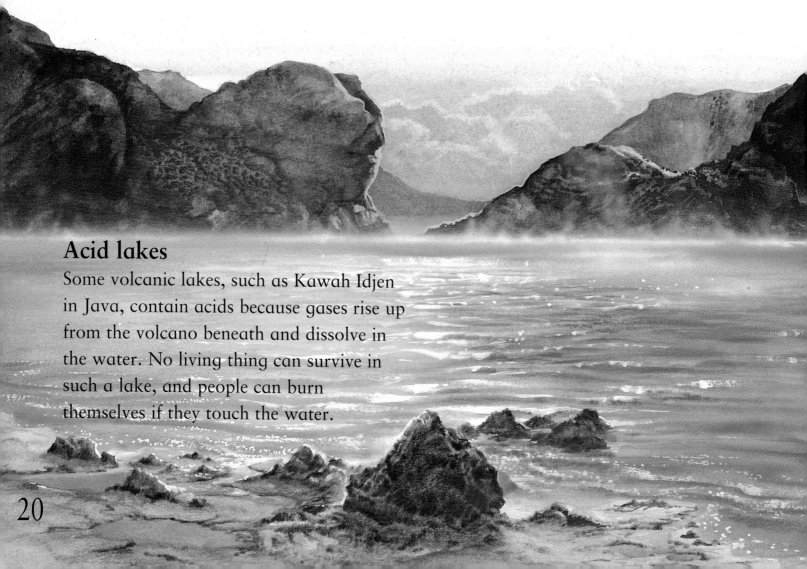

Volcanic activity can completely change the landscape. Some volcanoes erupt with such force that they blow their tops off. This leaves huge craters, which can fill with rainwater to form large lakes, many metres above sea level. Other volcanoes collapse inwards and form craters called calderas, which gradually fill with water.

Crater lake

After a volcano has erupted, its vent, or pipe, is blocked by a plug of solid magma. This lets rainwater collect in the crater, forming a lake.

Acid lakes

Some volcanic lakes, such as Kawah Idjen in Java, contain acids because gases rise up from the volcano beneath and dissolve in the water. No living thing can survive in such a lake, and people can burn themselves if they touch the water.

How a caldera lake is formed

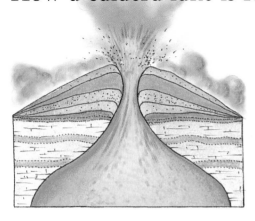 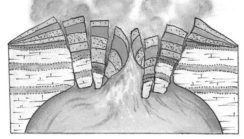 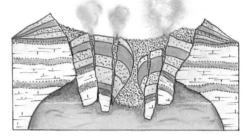

1 Underneath an active volcano, there is a large chamber that is full of liquid magma.

2 During an eruption, the level of magma in this chamber can drop. This causes the volcano walls to collapse into it, forming a giant crater, or caldera.

3 After the eruption, this caldera can fill with rainwater to form a lake. New, smaller volcanoes may form inside the caldera.

Scientists testing the levels of acid in the lake

Major eruptions

Plaster cast of Pompeii victim

Every year, at least 60 volcanoes erupt somewhere in the world. Many eruptions are small, but some are huge and cause great damage. The eruption of Vesuvius in Italy in AD 79 buried the town of Pompeii in hot ash and cinders. People in nearby Herculaneum were also killed in the blast of hot ash and gas.

Pompeii

Ash set hard like cement around the people killed in Pompeii. Their bodies decayed inside and left hollows. Many years later, scientists filled these with plaster, and made casts of the bodies.

Famous volcanic eruptions

Krakatau, 1883

A volcano blew this island in Indonesia to pieces. People heard the explosion 4,000km away, and the ash in the sky made the Moon and Sun look green.

Katmai, 1912

When Mount Katmai in Alaska exploded, a huge area was covered in a thick layer of ash. Luckily, not many people were killed, as only a few lived nearby.

Pinatubo, 1991

Mount Pinatubo in the Philippines erupted after 600 years. The huge clouds of ash and dust blocked out the Sun, and buried villages and fields for kilometres.

Vesuvius, AD 79
The eruption of Vesuvius is probably the most famous volcanic explosion ever. The remains of the people killed in the huge blast lay undiscovered for 1,700 years.

After the eruption

A volcanic eruption completely changes people's lives and the place where they live.

Cities, towns and the surrounding countryside are destroyed. A huge eruption can change the world's weather for months or even years. The ash and dust in the air can block out the Sun and make the climate colder.

Homes destroyed
When a volcano erupts, many people lose their homes and everything that they own.

Before the eruption...
Mount St Helens in the United States was a peaceful snow-topped mountain for 123 years before it erupted in May 1980.

Car crusher

An erupting volcano throws out blocks of lava and smaller lumps of lapilli and ash. Large rocks travelling at great speed can kill people and crush cars.

New growth

Twenty years after the eruption, new trees are growing, replacing those that were destroyed in the explosion of 1980.

...and after

The eruption of Mount St Helens completely blew away the north side of the mountain. All that was left was a dome of solid magma with a jagged crater of rock around it. The mountain was 400m shorter.

Living on a volcano

Volcanoes are usually dangerous places, but they can also be useful to people who live near them. Volcanic ash is full of minerals that feed the soil and make it better for growing crops. Sulphur and other minerals are mined to use in factories. Water is heated underground by red-hot magma, and it can be used to power turbines for electricity, or to heat homes and supply hot water to people living in the area.

Hot land of ice!

Iceland contains many volcanoes, as well as hot springs and geysers. Hydrothermal (hot water) power stations supply nearly half of Iceland's electricity. People can bathe in the open-air hot springs which are rich in minerals, and good for their health.

Hydrothermal power station

People relaxing in the Blue Lagoon, Iceland

Volcanic wheat

The Greek island of Santorini is on the edge of a large crater that was formed after a huge eruption in 1645 BC. Wheat and other crops grow well in the rich soil.

The lake of hot water is full of minerals

Studying volcanoes

The science of volcanoes is known as volcanology. Volcanologists study volcanoes so that they can tell when and how they might erupt, and they record details of the eruptions. They work in scientific laboratories, but they sometimes have to visit the actual volcano, while it is erupting.

Extreme heat

Volcanologists wear special suits to keep out the intense heat of the volcano. The suits are very bulky and make moving about difficult.

Volcanologists measuring the heat of the lava during an eruption

The right equipment

Volcanologists use special tools to measure and record what happens on a volcano. These tools must be light, so that they can be carried easily. They must also be strong enough to stand up to great heat.

Long metal rod to scoop up hot lava

Compass for surveying and mapping a volcano

Binoculars to look at an erupting volcano from a safe distance

Tape to measure if cracks in the volcano are getting wider

Thermometer to measure the temperature of lava

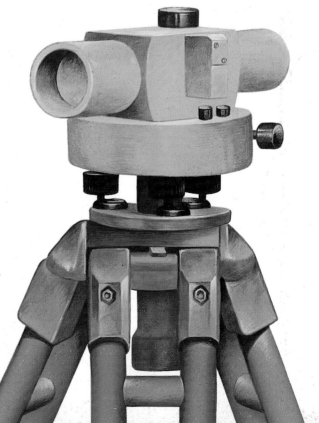

Laser-guided level to show if magma pushing up from underground is making the sides of a volcano bulge

Volcanoes in space

There are volcanoes on many of the moons and planets in our solar system. The Earth's Moon has many volcanoes, and so does Mars, but all of these are now extinct. Venus, Jupiter, and possibly Uranus, have active volcanoes. These volcanoes are usually large, and they erupt often and with great force. Jupiter's volcanoes throw out sulphur rather than lava.

Olympus Mons

Mount Everest

Record-breaker

The largest-ever volcano is not on Earth but on the planet Mars. Olympus Mons is extinct and is three times taller than Mount Everest, the highest mountain on Earth.

The eruption of Io

In 1979, the US spacecraft *Voyager I* flew past Io, one of the 16 moons of Jupiter. At the time, the volcano Prometheus was throwing out a fountain of gases 160km into space above the moon's surface.

Glossary

aa Jagged, crumbly lava.

active volcano A volcano that has erupted quite recently and may erupt again.

ash Fine pieces of lava thrown out of a volcano during an eruption. Very fine pieces are called volcanic dust.

caldera Large crater or bowl at the top of a volcano.

core The centre of the Earth, a metal ball of iron and nickel. The inner core is solid, but the outer core is made up of liquid metals – iron and nickel.

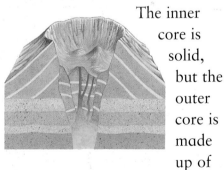

crater The hole at the top of a volcano's vent that is often filled with water.

crust The hard outer shell of the Earth that floats on top of the mantle (layer of hot rock).

crystal A solid mineral formed as molten lava cools or as liquid evaporates into the air.

dormant volcano A volcano that has not erupted for centuries, but might do so again.

extinct volcano A volcano that is dead and will never erupt again.

fissure A crack in the Earth's surface.

hot spot A thin part of the Earth's crust, where magma burns through to form a volcano.

lapilli Little stones of lava thrown out of a volcano during an explosion.

lava Hot, molten rock that erupts from a volcano.

magma Extremely hot, molten rock which comes from the Earth's mantle.

magma chamber A large chamber beneath the volcano which fills up with magma before an eruption.

mantle The soft part of the Earth that lies between the outer core and the crust. The mantle is hot and, in places, is molten.

mineral A chemical, made up of elements, found in all rocks.

pahoehoe A hot, runny lava that looks like coils of rope when it cools down.

plate A slowly moving section of the Earth's crust.

plug A lump of cool, solid magma that fills the vent of the volcano beneath its crater.

vent Pipe formed from cracks inside the volcano, out of which magma erupts.

volcanologist A person who studies volcanoes (also known as a vulcanologist).

Index

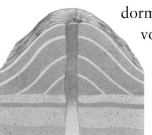